CELEBRATION OF LIFE

A Ten-Step Planning Guide

By

Sarah F. D. Hamm
and
Harriet Spradley Thompkins

This book is a work of non-fiction. Names and places have been changed to protect the privacy of all individuals. The events and situations are true.

First published by AuthorHouse 01/06/05

ISBN: 1-4184-8438-5 (e-book)
ISBN: 1-4184-5165-7 (Paperback)
ISBN: 1-4184-5166-5 (Dust Jacket)

This book is printed on acid free paper.

Clearwater, FL 33757
Printed in the U.S.A

Poem for survivors

Do not stand at my grave and weep.
I am not there. I do not sleep.
I am a thousand winds that blow.
I am the diamond glints on snow.
I am the sunlight on ripened grain.
I am the gentle autumn rain.
When you awake in the morning's hush
I am the soft uplifting rush
Of quiet birds in circling flight.
I am the star that shines at night.
Do not stand at my grave and cry
I am not there. I did not die.
Anonymous

Dedication

To our Lord and Savior Jesus Christ, family and friends.

Count your blessings, not your troubles,
And you'll make it through what comes along.
Within you are so many answers,
Understand, have courage, be strong.

Preface

Those Who Loved Me

Now I am gone, release me and let me go. I have so many things to see and do. You mustn't toe yourself to me with tears. Be happy that we had so many years. I gave you my love and you can only guess how much you gave to me in happiness. I thank you for the love you each showed, but it's time I travel alone. So grieve awhile for me if you must. Then let your grief be comforted by trust. It's only for a while that we must part. So bless the memories within your heart. I won't be far away for life goes on. So if you need me, call and I will come. Tho' you can't see or touch me, I will be near. If you listen with your heart you will hear all of my love around you soft and clear, and then, when you must come this way alone, I'll greet you with smile and say, "Welcome home".

Learn to make the most of life,
Lose no happy day.

Time can never bring you back
Chances swept away.

Leave no tender word unsaid,
Love while life shall last.

The mill will never turn again,
With water that has passed.

Table of Contents

Lord God,

The path of life is often difficult, I ask not you make it smooth, but to light it so that I can see to walk in love. If for a moment the light is dim, let me walk by faith, trusting you with each step I take. Amen

Introduction

Blessed are they that mourned: for they shall be comforted ~Matthew 5:4~

We know how unprepared most people are when a death occurs. That is why we decided to write this 10-step guide. Making funeral arrangements can be overwhelming and grief numbing. Within 24 hours after death, the family must make many decisions. Clear and strenuous choices can be difficult to make. When you take the time to make these choices now, you will spare your family the added burden, both financial and emotional, of having to make decisions on your behalf.

The best gift you can give your family is to make your wishes known in writing. This guide is design to give you peace of mind for the benefit of your family. You are doing this for them. More family disputes arise following a death than almost any time in our lives. Emotions are at a peak and venting them occurs at inappropriate times.

Prepay your funeral expenses, or make sure you have a designated life insurance policy for this expense. Meet with your local funeral director and find out what expenses to expect and the best way to take care of this obligation. Don't leave your final ceremony to someone else. After all they are celebrating your life.

We hope that you will use *Celebration of Life* as a guide to create a meaningful memorial. We hope that the information you have included in this guide will provide valuable memories to your survivors.

It is a good idea to review the contents of this guide periodically with whoever will be carrying out your wishes. This review will make sure that your intentions are current and up-to-date.

If you feel uncomfortable about using *Celebration of Life* and planning ahead of your death, it's okay. When you are ready, take a few minutes to browse the contents. You will be surprise how your attitude will change and how positive you will feel about reflecting on your life's story.

Remember that you are giving your love ones a gift. This guide will help them to know that you were able to face this difficult matter. It also will bring a comfort to them to know that they are carrying out your "life's celebration" the way you would have wanted. It's okay.

~*Harriet & Sarah*~

Lord God

Thank you for making me special.
I feel so special when I experience your love.
I know that you are preparing
A place in heaven for me.
To be considered your child is overwhelming,
As I am chosen to be part of your family.
I long for your presence,
Laying crown at your feet,
And worshipping you forever.
Amen

Step 1

Locate a Funeral Home

"To everything there is a season, and a time to every purpose under the heaven. A time to be born and a time to die."

~Ecclesiastes 3:1&2~

Death is a fact of life and there is simply no way to avoid it. Indeed there is "A time to be born and a time to die." Through a funeral, we pay our last respects and celebrate the life of our departed loved one.

Choose a Funeral Home

If there is more than one funeral home in your area, you want to find out what services are offered. You may be interested in one that caters to your particular religion, cultural, traditions or fraternal organization. Visit or call the funeral homes in your

1

area and decide which can better personalize your desired service.

If you want a service to be held in another location or state, you will need to specify and complete the proper paperwork with your local funeral home.

Complete the following:

(Local within your city/town)

Funeral Home_____

Name of Director_____

Address_____

City_____

Telephone Number _____

Celebration of Life

Services to be held at another location or State
(Local funeral director will also be required)

Funeral Home_____

_____

Name of Director_____

_____

Address_____

_____

City_____

Telephone Numbers_____

_____

Sarah F. D. Hamm and Harriet Spradley Thompkins

*F*aith

Faith sees the invisible,
Believes the unbelivable,
And receives the impossible.
~Corrie Ten Boom~

Step 2

Prepare the Important Papers

"Lift up your heads, O ye gates; even lift them up, ye everlasting doors; and the King of glory shall come in." Psalms 24:8

I f the following information is in a safety deposit box, be sure someone has copies. Someone should be aware of and able to locate this information.

Veteran Benefits
 (Funeral director will contact Veteran Administration)

Branch Affiliation_____

_____

Serial Number_____
Rank_____

Veteran Benefits (Continued)

Papers are kept _____
_____

Retirement Insurance
(Pension, social security, union, fraternal order, etc.)

_____
_____
_____
_____
_____
_____
_____

Insurance Companies names policy numbers, and agent name.
(Have there been changes made in your life insurance since you purchased this insurance?)

Company Name_____
Policy number_____

Company Name_____
Policy number_____

Your Will
(To be drawn up by an attorney and a copy left with a trusted person)

Person's Name_____
Telephone number_____
Attorney_____

_____
Telephone number_____

Bank Accounts
(Names, Location and account numbers)

Checking_____
Address_____

_____
Telephone number_____

Savings_____
Address_____
Telephone number_____

Credit Union_____
Address_____
Telephone number_____

Safety Deposit Box Location
(Key) Some deposit boxes are sealed for a period of time.

_____

_____

_____

_____

Stocks and Bonds (Other than safety deposit box)

_____

_____

_____

_____

Other Important Papers/Special Instructions
(Items someone should be aware of and able to locate)

_____

_____

_____

_____

Step 3

Decide on Prepaid Funeral Arrangements

"And as it is appointed unto men once to die."
~Hebrews 9:27~

The benefits of prearrangement means every detail can be arranged according to your desires. The arrangement will save your family from any additional burdens at a time of emotional stress and to spare them from financial worry at a time of need.

Basic Prepaid Arrangements

The funeral home's basic services fee often include
- Embalming (preparing the body)
- Dressing the body
- Hairdressing and make-up
- Funeral home rental for the viewing and visitation or service

Basic Prepaid Arrangements (Continued)

- Use of hearse to transport the body to the funeral site (church) cemetery and use of vehicles to transport the immediate family.
- Costs of the casket
- Director's First Call
- Viewing before or after the service (optional)
- Other funeral details and services

Most prepaid services contract is honored by any funeral home. The contract will be based on current prices. Payment plans are available to fit your budget. For more information on prepaid funeral services, contact your local funeral home.

Inform the funeral director if you have a Prepaid Funeral Plan

Name of the Company of the Prepaid Service

_____

_____

Address_____

_____

_____

Phone Number_____

Policy Number_____

Sarah F. D. Hamm and Harriet Spradley Thompkins

Everything that happens
is part of God's eternal plan.
Today what seems a mystery
in time we'll understand.
Remember prayers are with you
to give you strength today.
Call on those of us who love you
to share with you along the way.
When trouble comes, we often say,
"Why did this have to be?"
But blessings come in many ways
that sometimes we can't see.

Step 4

Plan the Service

"Therefore we are always confident. Knowing that, whilst we are at home in the body. We are absent from the Lord; we are confident, I say, and willing rather to be absent from the body, and to be present with the Lord."

~II Corinthians 5:6&8~

The celebrating (funeral) services of today vary greatly from the traditional services of years past. A funeral can and should be as unique as the life that is being celebrated.

Types of Service

Complete Funeral Service – Full Service
- Viewing and visitation at the funeral home
- Use of hearse to transport the body to funeral site and cemetery
- Use of vehicles to transport the family
- Cemetery plot
- Cost of casket
- Your personalized program (See Step 6)
- Viewing before or after the service
- Newspaper obit

Memorial Service
- No Viewing
- Your personalized program (Step 6)
- Memorial table or picture board (optional)

Graveside Service – No Viewing
- No program
- Short program at gravesite (Step 6)

No Services
- Cremation and no program
- Burial without program

Cremation
- Full service with program after cremation
- Viewing prior to cremation with program
- No service

Selecting a Casket

This is included in the prepaid funeral program or can be handled separate

Details in design, construction and finish are meant to enhance the casket in an attractive and dignified manner. It helps keep the tasks of handling, closing, and transporting to a smooth minimum. The Director will be able to offer selection in
- Metal caskets (stainless steel)
- Wood caskets (hardwood)
- Cremation caskets
- Orthodox caskets (religious ceremonies)
- Urns

For more information, contact your local funeral home or local casket companies.

If you have selected a casket, complete the following:

Company_____

Address:_____

_____

Telephone Number_____

How to Spend Your Dash

I read of a man who stood to speak at the funeral of a friend.
He referred to the dates on her tombstone from the beginning to
the end...
He noted that first came the date of her birth, the date that
followed brought tears.
But he said what mattered most of all was the dash between
those years.
That dash represents all of the time spent alive on earth... Now
only those who loved her know what that little line is worth.
For it matters not how much we own;
the cars, the house, the cash.
What matters is how we live and love and how we spend our
dash.

So think about this long and hard;
are there things that you'd like to change?
For you never know how much time is left; you could be a dash
midrange.
If we could just slow down long enough to find out what is true
and real,
and always try to understand the way other people feel.

17

Sarah F. D. Hamm and Harriet Spradley Thompkins

To be less quick to anger and show appreciation more.
To love people in ours lives we've never loved before.
We'd treat each other with respect and more often wear a smile.
Remembering that special dash will only last a while.

When your eulogy is being read with your lives actions to rehash...
Would you be proud of the things they say about how you spent your DASH?

Author Unknown

When I Must Leave You

When I must leave you for a little while
Please do not grieve and shed wild tears,
And hug your sorrow to you through the years.
But start out bravely with a gallant smile;
And for my sake and in my name,
Live on and do all things the same.
Feed not your loneliness on empty days,
But fill each waking hour in useful ways.
Reach out your hand in comfort and in cheer,
And in turn will comfort you,
And hold you near.
And never, never be afraid to die,
For I am waiting for you in the sky!

Sarah F. D. Hamm and Harriet Spradley Thompkins

Step 5

Write the Obituary

"No one was ever honored for what they received. Honor has been the reward for that they gave."
Calvin Coolidge

Obituary often times becomes just a list of facts. Many unique things about you are left out because the family is under emotional stress and unprepared. Make your obituary interesting by reflecting on a life lived and enjoyed. Include activities, accomplishments, events and things that were important to you.

Newspaper Obit

Provide a list of newspapers other than your local you would like to have your obituary appear in. This will be a short version of your past. The Director will assist you with what is required for the newspaper. –See Sample in Appendix D

21

Sarah F. D. Hamm and Harriet Spradley Thompkins

Newspaper Obit (Continued)

Do you want a picture in the newspaper? (If the answer is yes, where is the picture located?)

_____

_____

_____

_____

_____

_____

The human spirit is stronger than anything that can happen to it.
~George C. Scott~

Program Obit

This will be a part (more detailed than the Newspaper Obituary) of the program.

_____

_____

_____

_____

_____

_____

_____

_____

_____

_____

_____

_____

_____

_____

_____

_____

_____

_____

_____

_____

Program Obit (Continued)

_____

_____

_____

_____

_____

_____

_____

_____

_____

_____

_____

_____

_____

_____

_____

_____

_____

_____

_____

_____

_____

_____

_____

_____

Celebration of Life

Your presence is a gift to the world,
You're unique and one of a kind.
Your life can be what you want it to be -
Take it one day at a time.

Count your blessings, not your troubles,
And you'll make it through what comes along.
Within you are so many answers,
Understand, have courage, be strong.

Sarah F. D. Hamm and Harriet Spradley Thompkins

Step 6

Develop the Program

"Those who bring sunshine to the lives of others cannot keep it from themselves."

~James Matthew Barrie~

The program should be as unique as the life that is being celebrated. Don't think you must have a traditional program or that your ideas for a special ceremony are unacceptable.

Do you want a picture on the program?
If the answer is yes, where is the picture located?

_____

_____

Visitation/Viewing
- Public – Before service or after service
- Private
- No viewing
- See *Step 4* for arrangement and type of service

Sarah F. D. Hamm and Harriet Spradley Thompkins

When you were born, you were crying and everyone around you was smiling. Live your life so that when you die, you're the one who is smiling and everyone around you is crying.

Pallbearers include contact information (Six)

1. _____
2. _____
3. _____
4. _____
5. _____
6. _____

Services to be held at (Church, Chapel, etc.)

Name_____

Address_____

Phone_____

Officiated by

Name_____

Address_____

Phone_____

Eulogist

_____

_____

Invocation or Prayer:

_____

_____

Sarah F. D. Hamm and Harriet Spradley Thompkins

Reflections   Yes_____   No_____

Happiness lies for those who cry, those who hurt, those who have searched, and those who have tried, for only they can appreciate the importance of people who have touched their lives. Love begins with a smile, grows with a kiss and ends with a tear. The brightest future will always be based on a forgotten past, you can't go on well in life until you let go of your past failures and heartaches.

Music
(You may want a piano, organ, guitar, flute or another musical instrument.) What kind of music do you prefer?

_____
_____
_____
_____

You may want a group of friends, relatives, choir or soloist to sing. Name them here. How many selections?

_____
_____
_____
_____

Favorite Song

_____
_____
_____

Flowers
Do you prefer to send memorials to your favorite charities? If yes, list them

_____

Dream what you want to dream; go where you want to go; be what you want to be, because you have only one life and one chance to do all the things you want to do.

Preferred Scriptures, Poems, or Psalms

_____
_____
_____
_____
_____
_____
_____
_____
_____
_____
_____
_____
_____
_____

Other items you can include in the Service or Program

Memorial Table/Pictures Board (Bulletin/Memory Board). Items you would like placed on the table and location.

_____
_____
_____

_____

Pictures you would like in the collage and location.

_____

_____

_____

_____

_____

Tribute Video Yes_____ No _____

May you have enough happiness to make you sweet, enough trials to make you strong, enough sorrow to keep you human, enough hope to make you happy.

Sarah F. D. Hamm and Harriet Spradley Thompkins

Step 7

Decide on What to Wear

Flatter me, and I may not believe you. Criticize me, and I may not like you. Ignore me, and I may not forgive you. Encourage me, and I will not forget you."

~William Arthur Ward~

D escribe the clothing you want to wear. Use a special clothes hanger to specify your selections or list someone special to shop for you. Select a complete outfit including underwear, stockings, socks, tie and shoes.

Instructions:

_____

_____

_____

_____

_____

_____

_____

_____

_____

_____

How do you want your hair styled?

Usually the funeral staff includes a
beautician/barber. (Attached a picture if possible)
Instructions:

_____

_____

_____

_____

_____

_____

_____

_____

_____

Make-up Instructions

_____

_____

_____

_____
_____
_____
_____
_____

Fingernails Polished. Yes_____ No_____ If yes, what color?

_____
_____
_____
_____

Do you want to wear jewelry? Yes_____ No_____ If yes, describe here.

_____
_____
_____
_____
_____
_____

Do want your glasses? On _____Off____

Sarah F. D. Hamm and Harriet Spradley Thompkins

The happiest of people don't necessarily have the best of everything; they just make the most of everything that comes along their way.

Step 8

Select Final Resting Place and Grave Marker

"O death, where is thy sting? O grave, where is thy victory? But thanks be to God, which giveth us the victory through our Lord Jesus Christ."

~ *I Corinthians 15:55,57*~

One of the most difficult things a family faces is making a trip to the cemetery to select a plot or you may designate your funeral director to choose a plot for you. Choosing and purchasing your final resting place is another act of love that you can accomplish long before the need arises. The mobile society of today makes this decision very difficult for the family. You may prefer where you expire, burial near family members possibly in another state, maybe your hometown. This is not an easy choice to make without guidance from your funeral director.

Cemetery

Some cemeteries give you choice of earth burial or to be entombed above the ground or a mausoleum. If this is a choice you want to consider, you will need to inquire at the cemeteries of choice to see if a mausoleum is available and what the requirements are. Most cemeteries also have designated religious sections, veteran's section that you may wish to consider.

Name_____

Address_____

_____

Phone _____

Earth Burial_____

Mausoleum_____

If purchased – Location and where paperwork can be found:

_____

_____

_____

Grave Marker

Contact

_____

_____

_____

_____

Inscriptions

_____

_____

_____

_____

_____

_____

_____

_____

_____

_____

_____

Sarah F. D. Hamm and Harriet Spradley Thompkins

Memory

As I watch the rain
Gently falling down,
I think of how much
I wish you were around.
But since for now
That is not meant to be,
I'll be content
With your memory.

Step 9

Plan the Repast

"He that is of a merry heart hath a continual feast" ~Proverbs 15:15~

A fter the service and the interment, family and friends gather a final time in the decease honor. Usually this is a time a large meal is served and others console the family. Generally, others and the family supply the food.

Location
(Place, church annex, hall, etc.)

_____

_____

_____

_____

_____

_____

_____

_____

47

Sarah F. D. Hamm and Harriet Spradley Thompkins

Gather ye rosebuds while ye may, old time is still a flying: and this same flower that smiles today, tomorrow maybe dying. ~ Carpe Diem Seize the Day~

Menu

_____

_____

_____

_____

_____

_____

_____

_____

_____

_____

_____

_____

_____

_____

_____

_____

_____

_____

_____

_____

_____

_____

_____

_____

Sarah F. D. Hamm and Harriet Spradley Thompkins

The dead sing of nothing but love.
~Patrick Friesen~

Step 10

Give Special Instruction/Notification

A man is not remembered for what he took but for what he gave. ~Sir Winton Churchill~

Take time to jot down simple messages to those you care about. Put them with this workbook. What a lasting remembrance these will be. If you have special personal belongings that you want someone to have as a special memory (items that don't need to be in a will), this is a good place to make note.

_____
_____
_____
_____
_____
_____
_____
_____
_____
_____
_____

How would I like to be remembered?

_____

_____

_____

_____

_____

_____

_____

_____

_____

People to Notify:

_____

_____

_____

_____

_____

_____

_____

Organization(s) To Notify (Any organization, club, church auxiliary or affiliation)

_____

_____

_____

_____

_____

_____

_____

_____

_____

_____

"For we brought nothing into this world, and it is certain that we can carry nothing out." ~I Timothy 6:7~

Sarah F. D. Hamm and Harriet Spradley Thompkins

Life is sweet, just because of
friends we have made
and the things which in common we share.
We want to live on, not because of ourselves,
but because of the people who care.

Declaration of Intent

I_____

have given careful thought and consideration to the choices I have made and outlined in this book. I understand that this is not legally binding and that my family and/or other appropriate persons, based on the circumstances at the time of my death, will make the ultimate decision.

I request that my wishes be fulfilled to the extent possible.

Date: _____

Signed by: _____

Witness by: _____

Witness by: _____

Sarah F. D. Hamm and Harriet Spradley Thompkins

We make the world in which we live
By what we gather and what we give,
By our daily deeds and the things we say,
By what we keep or we cast away.
We make our world by the beauty we see
In a skylark's song or lilac tree,
In a butterfly's wing, in the pale moons' rise,
And the wonder that lingers in midnight skies.
We make our world by the life we lead,
By the friends we have, by the books we read,
By the pity we show in the hour of care,
By the loads we lift and the love we share.
We make our world by the goals we pursue,
By the heights we seek and the higher view,
By hopes and dreams that reach the sun
And a will to fight till the heights are won.
What is the place in which we dwell,
A hut or a palace, a heaven or hell
We gather and scatter, we take and we give,
We make our world—and there we live.
~A.G. Walton~

If Tomorrow Starts Without Me

If tomorrow starts without me,
And I'm not there to see,
If the sun should rise and find your eyes
All filled with tears for me;
I wish so much you wouldn't cry
The way you did today,
While thinking of the many things,
We didn't get to say.
I know how much you love me,
As much as I love you,
And each time that you think of me,
I know you'll miss me too;
But when tomorrow starts without me,
Please try to understand,
That an angel came and called my name,
And took me by the hand,

Sarah F. D. Hamm and Harriet Spradley Thompkins

And said my place was ready,
In heaven far above,
And that I'd have to leave behind
All those I dearly love.
But as I turned to walk away,
A tear fell from my eye
For all my life, I'd always thought,
I didn't want to die.
I had so much to live for,
So much left yet to do,
It seemed almost impossible,
That I was leaving you.

I thought of all the yesterdays,
The good ones and the bad,
The thought of all the love we shared,
And all the fun we had.
If I could relive yesterday,
Just even for a while,
I'd say good-bye and kiss you
And maybe see you smile.
But then I fully realized,
That this could never be,
For emptiness and memories,
Would take the place of me.

Celebration of Life

And when I thought of worldly things,
I might miss come tomorrow,
I thought of you, and when I did,
My heart was filled with sorrow.
But when I walked through Heaven's gates,
I felt so much at home.
When God looked down and smiled at me,
From His great golden throne,

He said, "This is eternity,
And all I've promised you."
Today your life on earth is past,
But here life starts anew.
I promise no tomorrow,
But today will always last,
And since each day's the same way
There's no longing for the past.
You have been so faithful,
So trusting and so true.
Though there were times you did
Some things you knew you shouldn't do.

But you have been forgiven
And now at last you're free.
So won't you come and take my hand
And share my life with me?
So when tomorrow starts without me,
Don't think we're far apart,

Sarah F. D. Hamm and Harriet Spradley Thompkins

For every time you think of me,
I'm right here, in your heart.
~ Author Unknown ~

Appendix A

Frequently Asked Questions

(FAQs)

- What are some benefits of planning your own arrangements?

- Can making your own arrangements be a positive experience?

- What are some factors to consider with choosing a funeral director?

- What are some factors to consider with choosing a funeral director?

- What is the role of the funeral director?

- What is the difference between a funeral service and a memorial service?

- What does disposition of body mean?

- What are some burial choices available?

- Why people choose burial?

- What are some decisions you must make if you choose burial?

- What is cremation?

- What are some cremation choices?

- Why people choose cremation?

- What decisions you must make if you choose cremation?

- What is a wake?

- What does viewing the body means?

- What are columbariums?

- What are the laws on ash scattering?

FAQs Answers

What are some benefits of planning your own arrangements?

- Let's surviving family members know what type of funeral service arrangements you would like.
- Saves the family stress.
- Provides an opportunity to personalize the funeral and post-death activities.
- Reassures survivors won't select a type of funeral different than the one desired.
- Assures a surviving spouse of having the same funeral as the one selected for the deceased spouse, if desired.
- Avoids the problems of family separation.
- Gives peace of mind to the person planning his or her funeral in advance.
- Organizes personal records in one place.
- Eliminates financial concerns and decisions at the time when the family is in distress when you prepay.

Can making your own arrangements be a positive experience?

For most people, death is a taboo subject and not something that is usually discussed. The thought of planning a funeral is not generally at the forefront of people's mind, but there is a new way of thinking on this. Creating your own funeral that is both personal and appropriate to the individual is now on the increase.

If you don't do anything about the final arrangements then close relatives have to try and decide on the appropriate arrangement that the funeral will take. This is at a time when they are most distressed and least able to cope. The other potential problem is that the funeral is unsatisfactory or inappropriate because it does not reflect the values and beliefs of the person life who has died.

What are some factors to consider with choosing a funeral director?

Funeral directors will manage funeral arrangements and give advice and support. Ask if the funeral director you choose belongs to a trade association. Encourage him/her to provide full information about their services and prices.

These factors may influence your choice:
- Location of the firm's premises.
- Range of services provided.
- The way you are treated by the staff.
- Cost.
- Recommendation of those who have used the service.
- Ownership (small family business or large firm).
- Size of establishment (can it accommodate your family)
- Resourceful knowledge of businesses that you may need after funeral service.
- Experience

What is the role of the funeral director?

- A high level of professionalism and experience.
- Make all the necessary arrangements.
- Provide appropriate staff.
- Provide a selection of coffins.
- Transfer the deceased from the place of death to the funeral director's premises.
- Care for the deceased prior to the funeral.

- Provide a hearse to the nearest cemetery or crematorium.
- Provide necessary transportation for family and deceased.
- Arrange for burial or cremation as requested.
- Know all the national and state laws
- Submit all necessary paperwork that required by law.

What is the difference between a funeral service and a memorial service?

A funeral service is one in which the body is present.
At a memorial service, it is not.
Sometimes it is necessary to have a funeral in one place, and then to have a memorial service later someplace else.
At most funerals, a member of the clergy presides. The casket is usually closed during the service, although it may be opened at the end for a viewing or most commonly viewing before the service.
Your decision will be indicated in Steps 4 and 6.

What does disposition of body mean?

Disposition is the term used by the funeral industry to describe the final handling of the deceased's remains.

Although your initial decision for the disposition of the body is between burial and cremation, there are several variations on each.

Whichever choice you make, the body will eventually return to its natural elements.

What are some burial choices available?

If the body is buried ...
1. It can be interred (earth burial).
2. It can be entombed in a crypt within a mausoleum (above-ground burial).
3. It can be buried at sea.
4. It can be sprinkle in other ways and places.

Why people choose burial?

Although the trend is moving toward cremation, the majority of North Americans still choose to bury their dead and to be buried themselves. Here are some reasons you might choose burial.

• Burial is traditional within some families, religious group, or geographical area
For instance, in the United States today, about 79 percent choose burial. In Canada, the rate is about 64 percent.
• You do not like the idea of the body being "burned"
• You want to erect a monument on the grave
Perhaps you want to visit the grave in the days to come, and you find a graveyard more appealing than say, a columbarium.

What are some decisions you must make if you choose burial?

o Which kind of casket (or coffin)
o Which cemetery to use
o What kind of plot
o What to put on the gravestone
o How close to a family member you can purchase a plot

What is cremation?

Decomposition of the body in the earth (after burial) is the slow oxidation of the body tissues.

Cremation, on the other hand, provides rapid oxidation.

What are some cremation choices?

If the body is cremated …
1. The remains can be stored by the family — and perhaps kept on display — in an urn or other container.
2. You may take the remains in the simple urn supplied by the crematory and distribute ("scatter") them over the land or water.
3. The remains can be placed in a niche within a columbarium.
4. The remains can be buried in the ground in a regular plot or in a smaller cremation plot.
5. The remains can be entombed in a crypt within a mausoleum.

Why people choose cremation?

In the United States, in 1972, only five percent chose cremation. That number had quintupled by 1999, with over 25% choosing cremation.
The Cremation Association of North America predicts that by 2010, that figure will rise to 36%.

In Canada, the rate is already over 42%; in Great Britain, 71%; and over 98% in Japan.

Those who choose cremation (for themselves or others) often hold the belief that it is better to honor the memory of the person, not the dead body.

Here are some other reasons you might choose cremation:

• Cremation is traditional in your family, religious group, or geographical area

• You prefer the body to be returned quickly and cleanly to the elements

Many people believe that a cremated body becomes one with nature more quickly.

• **You have environmental concerns**

Perhaps you are worried about the use of valuable land for cemetery space, or believe it is wrong to fill the ground with materials that won't erode … metal coffins and concrete vaults.

• **You want to keep the costs down**

Selecting cremation does not mean, however, that you will have an inexpensive funeral.

You may still choose a casket and/or a viewing, and/or decide to have the cremated remains buried in the ground or placed in a columbarium.

You may still choose to be viewed which require rental of a casket. You don't need to bury the cremated remains in a casket.

What decisions you must make if you choose cremation?

• Who will do the cremation (a funeral home or a firm that specializes in direct cremation)
• Whether to use an urn or container
• What to do with the remains
    If you want distribution of the remains....
Some jurisdictions have laws prohibiting the scattering of remains; others require a permit. Ask your funeral director.

Also ask if there are any firms in your area that specialize in unique ways of distributing the remains, such as a plane to spread them over a mountain, or a ship to scatter them at sea.

Think of places that you especially loved close to home or far away or you choose the woods, a favorite lake, or on the old family farm.

Be sure to ask permission if you want to use private property.

What about using the remains to create new life, by planting a tree? Some survivors choose to mix the remains with the soil in flower beds and rose gardens at home. Every time the roses bloom, you will be reminded of your loved one.

If you decide to do this, however, consider what will happen if, some day, your family move away.
You might make this choice for pets, too. Our sweet old dog, Spot, is buried in the flower garden at our friend Leroy's house, a place where Spot spent happy hours lazing in the sun.

What is a wake?

The term wake is sometimes used to describe the reception before the funeral or memorial service. Traditionally, though, a wake means the friends and family keeping watch by the body before it is safely buried — especially through the night. (Hence the term "wake.")
In some families, there is much drinking and feasting and storytelling during the vigil.
For those who are comfortable with it, an informal storytelling session can be a wonderful way to remember the person.
The stories don't all have to be solemn, nor do they all have to show the person as a saint. We often love people as much for their flaws as for their strengths. Remember, too, that laughter is as much a sign of strong emotion as tears or anger.
And if the person had a good sense of humor, there are bound to be some funny stories.

This sharing can be a rich and powerful experience. You might even want to tape record this event to listen to again later.

What does viewing the body means?

Viewing means to have an open casket. The lid or the upper portion of the lid of the casket is left open so that mourners may take a last look at the deceased.

Many grief counselors feel that seeing the body helps mourners to accept that death has really occurred. And once the death has been accepted, healthy grieving can begin.

This may be especially important for those who had not seen the person for a while.

Your clergyperson may have his or her point of view on this question. Certainly members of your family will offer opinions.

Whatever you decide, it is unlikely you will please everyone. There are no clear-cut answers, and emotions can run high. Let your guiding principle, therefore, be what you feel is right in this situation. The circumstances of the death, the person's age, and the feelings of other mourners may all play a role in your decision.

What are columbariums?

Columbariums are vaults, or sometimes simply walls, with niches to store remains for those who have opted for cremation. The word comes from the Latin name for the dwelling place of a dove (columba), which Christians believe is the symbol of the Holy Spirit.

Some cemeteries have columbariums, which range from simple to ornate structures. Lately, there's a lot more interest in columbariums because more and more people are considering cremation. It's estimated that nationwide more than 25 percent of families nationwide choose cremation

In some regions, including California, Florida and the New England states, cremation rates are as high as 70 percent, says the society's Elvin Ellison. Some churches are building columbariums instead of the traditional church graveyard to take care of their departed faithful.

What are the laws on ash scattering?

Laws concerning ash scattering differ in each state. If state law permits it, ashes or cremains may be scattered in lieu of preserving them in a columbarium, burying them in a grave, or keeping them at home. Some cremation societies offer scattering services to their members.

Some people leave specific instructions on where they want their ashes scattered in a river, a pond or lake or some private property. Some prefer a hillside behind their homes. A golfer wanted his ashes strewn on his favorite fairway in his country club; one lady specified a rose garden.

Because it's expedient and inexpensive, ash scattering is beginning to appeal especially to busy and mobile families who can't always find time to visit a columbarium or a cemetery.

~

Learn to make the most of life,
Lose no happy day.

Time can never bring you back
Chances swept away.

Leave no tender word unsaid,
Love while life shall last.

The mill will never turn again,
With water that has passed.

~

Sarah F. D. Hamm and Harriet Spradley Thompkins

Appendix B

How to Write a Eulogy

What is a eulogy?

The term *eulogy* sounds stiff and formal, but eulogies can include simple reminiscences, war stories, or favorite jokes. A clergyman, pastor, minister, or etc usually performs this. However, this is strictly your decision. You may indeed write your own and name whom you want to deliver it.

Here's how to put the eulogy together:

1. Accumulate the facts
First, collect the biographical facts: your age, marriage dates, places lived, children, and so on. Now think about the stories you remember, or the turn of phrase or typical behavior that captures your character so well.
2. Select a theme
A theme gives unity to the eulogy, helping your listeners to see the rich patterns of your life. For

example, you may talk about the various roles you successfully played.

You the Businessperson, You the Family Member, and You the Winning Coach.

3. Organize the material

Write your notes in point form on sheets of paper or on 3x5 file cards - one idea to a card. Now group the cards into piles of similar topics. Then sort each pile of cards into a logical order.

4. Draft your speech

Write out the first draft. (If you have access to a computer, use it to make your editing job easier.) Use linking sentences to make each topic flow easily into the next. Pay most attention to your beginning and ending.

As you write and polish, keep the words "celebration" and "thanksgiving" in your mind. If it is appropriate, include a few moments of humor or lightheartedness.

Appendix C

The Obituary

What is an obituary notice?

An obituary notice has two functions: *Newspaper* and *Program*

Newspaper obituary purpose is:

1. To notify friends, distant family and colleagues of the death.

2. To give notice of which funeral home can be contacted for more information.

Some alternative functions could be:

1. Memorial donations information: "In lieu of flowers, donations may be made to ...."

2. List surviving members of the immediately family

Program Obituary gives a,
- o details biographical facts
- o brief synopsis of your life
- o list of accomplishments
- o list of immediate survivors
- o Organizations, clubs, committees, etc.

When to write the obituary?

Obituaries can be written at the time of death or before. Many people find it helpful to write their own obituary notice in advance for the following reasons:

1. The surviving family members might not remember, or struggle to find, specific dates (birth, employment, retirement, previous deaths).

2. They may not know proper spellings of people's names, places, companies or organizations.

3. They may not know all of your memberships in volunteer organizations and community clubs.

4. It could specify a favorite charity for donations that the surviving family wouldn't have thought of.

How should I write an obituary?

When a loved one dies, the family often leaves the writing of the obituary up to the funeral director with personal information. It is best to write the obituary yourself because you are the one that know you the best and know what is important to include and what is not.

When you are writing your obituary there are several important things to include. Mention what you did for a living. Even if you have been retired for many years, it is important to list your occupation. List any involvements you may have had, such as Lion's Club, volunteer fire department, or any clubs you may have participated in. List volunteer work and hobbies.

When listing surviving relatives, it is important to keep the list short and limited to the immediate family as there is not much space given to obituaries in the newspapers. The program obituary you may list more family members (See Step 6). Remember, many acquaintances are going to learn about your death by reading the obituary.

Check over the obituary with a fine-toothed comb, making sure there are no typos or grammatical mistakes; be sure to include your age, or birthday. If you lived in another town or state for a portion of your life, request a copy to be sent to the newspapers in the other towns to notify people who may have known you there.

People often save obituaries as remembrances of someone they loved, keep the newspaper obituary short but make sure it is something worthy of a scrap book and worthy of your memory. The program obituary will be more in length.

Appendix D

Newspaper Obituary

This order of listing is the format used by the newspapers. However, you may consult your local newspaper to confirm. The newspaper obituary should include information in Figure 1. Figure 2 is a sample of what the obituary looks like in the newspaper.

Figure 1. Information in Newspaper Obituary

Last name_____, First name_____, Middle initial_____. (Age#)*_____of (City of _____ demise)*_____, died (day of week)*_____ (list month, day and year)*_____ at (place of death)_____, i.e. Name of hospital, nursing home, rehabilitation, retirement home, etc. City of establishment*_____. He/she was born (city, state)_____ or he/she came here in (year) from (city)_____, (state)_____. (Place of employment and employer's name)_____ or (retired and company name)_____. Military history served as, rank, and branch _____. He/she was a member of (church name)_____or he/she was a Baptist, Methodist, and etc._____. Short list (for newspaper obit) of organizations, clubs, or volunteer groups that she/he was a member of _____. Survivors include his/her_____ spouse name_____, (number of sons) i.e. two sons/their names _____, city & state_____; (number of daughters) i.e. two daughters_____ their names_____ city & state_____; Parents if living_____ city & state _____; (# of brothers) two brothers_____, their names_____, city & state_____; (# of sisters) two sisters _____, their name_____, city & state_____; (# of grandchildren)* two grandchildren – not names in this obit; (# of great-grandchildren)* no names. Name of Funeral Home and City.

*Your love one or designee will fill these spaces at the time.

Figure 2. Sample Newspaper Obituary

Smith, John E, 72 of Largo, died Thursday (November 10, 1995) at Sunny Brook Nursing Home, Clearwater. He was born in Dawson, Ga., and came here in 1955. He retired from ABC Masonry Co. He was a Baptist. Survivors include a wife of 50 yrs., Sally. Two sons, Benjamin, Compton, CA;, Willie, Edison, Ga., one daughter Mildred, Washington, D.C. One brother Jimmie Fairfox, Va. Three grandchildren and four great-grandchildren. XYZ Funeral Home Dallas.

Sarah F. D. Hamm and Harriet Spradley Thompkins

Those who have lived a good life do not fear death,
but meet it calmly, and even long for it in the face of great
suffering.
But those who do not have a peaceful conscience, dread death as
though life means nothing but physical torment. The challenge is
to live our life
so that we will be prepared for death when it comes.

Appendix E

Program Obituary

Biographical facts – May include but certainly not limited to brief synopsis, and life accomplishments: Place in chronological order.

- Date of birth
- Parent (living or deceased)
- Educational background
- Acceptance of Jesus Christ/religious background
- Work experiences
- Marriage
- Military participation
- Other church involvement (communities, boards, auxiliaries, etc.)
- Organizations
- Awards
- Volunteer Service

He/she leaves to cherish his/her memories…

Sarah F. D. Hamm and Harriet Spradley Thompkins

Husband/Wife; (number of sons), Name each son(Wife name), city and state; (number of daughters), Name each daughter (Husband name), city and state; number of grandchildren; number of great-grandchildren. A host of nieces, nephews, cousins & friends.

~Life is full of special days — one right after the other.
All the special days in the past have brought us here today.
And all the special days to come, begin to take shape right now. Today is
indeed a special day, a sacred gift that is ours to fulfill .~

Appendix F

Sample Program

ORDER OF SERVICE

Totally your digression to include or exclude any of the below suggestions:
Officiator and presiding person may be different

- *Processional* (coming into the service) Choir singing *(See Step 6)*
    (Viewing coming in or at the end of service, refer to Step 4)
- *Selection* (See Step 6)
- *Invocation*… Name the person here
- *Scripture* Old Testament Name the person
    - New Testament Name the person
- *Selection/Solo*

- *Reflections/Tribute* (Optional you may choose to omit this part or you may name

who's to speak on what). (This can also determine the length of your service/program)[*] It is customary to limit tribute reflection to two (2) minutes.
- *Selection/Solo*
- *Acknowledgements/Resolutions* (usually the church clerk/secretary) (acknowledgements are located on the back cover of the program)
- *Poem*
- *Obituary Reading*
- *Solo/Selection*
- *Words of Comfort/Eulogy*
- *Recessional*
- *Benediction*

Is death the last step? No, it is the final awakening.

~Sir Walter Scott~

About the Authors

Sarah Hamm, is a Christian woman first, a wife, mother, grandmother, daughter, sister, friend, and a teacher by spirit. Sarah retired after nearly 32 years of employment with the government. She enjoys a busy and rewarding life with many church, community activities, and other volunteer efforts.

Harriet Spradley Thompkins loves the inspiration of God's Word. She loves participating in church activities, family reunions, and gospel singing events. She retired from the United States Coast Guard Reserves with 27 years of service. Harriet is a published poet and producer/host of a local awarding television show. She is a Librarian and the mother of one daughter.